ELIZABETHAN

IV

JONATHAN LOVEJOY

Jonathan Lovejoy

ii

ELIZABETHAN

The Complete Poems of Elizabeth Peele

Volume IV

Jonathan Lovejoy

Cover: *Back from the Fields,* 1898
William Adolphe Bouguereau (1825-1905)

ISBN-10: 0692319190
ISBN-13: 978-0692319192

For every Elizabeth

Introduction

Carmen Angelina Coletti (Elizabeth Peele) was perhaps the greatest composer who ever lived. After her death, studies of her music revealed a body of work—almost exclusively instrumental—of such beauty and power as to defy description. Even so, her lifelong reclusiveness rendered them obsolete to the world, and these musical treasures may remain apart from public view forever.

Even those few who heard her original scores did so in quiet apprehension, that this beautiful widow—lost somewhere deep in North Carolina farming country—brought forth music as completely ingenious as any ever written before. The sounds of greatness flowing from this woman's piano, surely this is not meant to be! For what purpose can she truly serve as a neoclassical composer in a jaded modern world, except as a curiosity and eventually, a fountain of eternal exploitation?

But while music did serve as a profession for her since she was twelve—her only wage being a sound mind and spirit—there was still another expression, both private and unintentional, equally meant for her eyes only. Gathered posthumously, so few of these "assemblies" can be called unique or special, and likely cannot set her apart from any other lonely poet in the world. But still they live on, as a glimpse into the mind of a musical genius and abused woman of Faith. Written parallel to her music over the years—with no striving for greatness or immortality—these poetic trifles, ironically, may be the only compositions of hers the world will ever hear.

Jonathan Lovejoy

ELIZABETHAN

or

"The Assemblies"

Volume IV

Jonathan Lovejoy

Such is the grandest music among us—

Poets...

Such are the wildest thoughts among us—

Composers...

The Book of Sarah

90th Assembly

451

Their father, drunk with greed and hypocrisy

Their mother, drunk with lust and pride

They sold their daughters to the wolves

For the price of wealth and riches

One daughter, who shines the morning sun

Hair, the color of silken gold

The other, whose earthen light is faded

With hair the color of tar

452

*V*anity drifts from times before

Entertwined in lost perversion

While spirits mouth riddles to the four winds

Prophesying a costly diversion

453

Eyes dark from years of grieving

Closed in peaceful eternal sleep

Now the widow begins her days bereaving

The loss of a tortured soul to weep

454

Beyond the woodlands
Past the road that goes to nowhere
There is a majestic mountain peak
Rising high above the grieving land

The snow covered slopes
Rise to a pinnacle
High above the distant horizon
Rising high upon the approach

No man can climb these mountain slopes
Towering above every soul in weeping
The dispossessed cannot even see the summit
Walking to and fro in ignorance

There are those among them
Knowledge given to a blessed few
These know to look to the far off place
Where the mountain rises high

Above the seed of devastation
Beneath the shores of heaven

Jonathan Lovejoy

There are those who look upon the Woodland Mountain

In the awe of understanding

They will look to the mountain once again

Underneath the Shores of Heaven

455

Sometimes there is a nobility

That goes beyond peace and serenity

Sometimes there is Battle…

And War for what is right

Remember the desert souls with Honor

With Understanding

Theirs is the cause of righteousness

A triumph of good over evil

91st Assembly

456

Warnings drift from times before
Exploding overhead
Drowning the world in bombs and fire
While we rest underneath the sea

Leaders expound their wisdom
Cloaked in greatness
While the foolish and the simple
Stumble about their merry way

Who can know the trouble when it gathers?
Who can bear it?
Who can sense the danger lying within…
Exploding all around?

Flames leap from the land to the sea
Rumbling the surface ineffectively
While we rest safely underneath
Watching them die

Elizabethan IV

They would love to see the Death of Democracy

Killed by our own feeble hands

By our own lack of judgment

But fate keeps us beneath the shelter…

To protect the cause of freedom

457

Even while poison threatens to flow

And death lays still all around me

The blonde maiden appears to give me hope

Promising a time of future prosperity

She is the maiden light

Sent to guide me through the dark'ned wilderness

From the shores of despair

To peace and serenity

Gather thyself, o faithful servant!

Consume this food fit for a king!

Wear thy colorful new raiment

Live the rest of thy days in the joy of happiness…

In the glory of a new life

458

The Earth is covered in a mist
A fog of dreams and tortured memories
Flowing around the trees of life
Knowing

In the mist grows lives of them who are lost
Lives of consequence
The living energy gathers in the mist
Bestowing melancholy among the dead

Tragedy, loss, pain
These are merely the beginning of sorrows
The rest is yet to come
Growing intrepidly from the mist

The mist is the fog of life
And death

From the Seed of Chaos the mist will grow
Rising to cover the trees of life
To cover the hills, the oceans…
And every mountain peak

Jonathan Lovejoy

To enshround the Earth in the Day of Recompense
In the comeuppance that is due

459

Poverty is a spirit

A curse bestowed upon mankind

There are those who try for generations

Trying to remove the stain of being poor

But we wrestle not against flesh and blood

But against principalities, rulers of the darkness of this world

Among the maladies they have placed upon us

Is the disease of poverty

Families sequestered in this prison by the millions

Even in the land of plenty

Because poverty is a curse…

A spirit sent to torment mankind

Those who have escaped poverty

Have done so by the Will of God

And that is all

Moaning…Mourning…Weeping in lamentation
Limping to and fro in filth
Calling for salvation, for deliverance from suffering
Hoping to be rescued from the stain of being poor

Poverty is a spirit
A curse bestowed upon mankind

460

Her promise shall rule Christendom

Carried upon the four winds

She will reign in every corner of the Earth

In the righteousness of God

Jonathan Lovejoy

92nd Assembly

461

Depression carries the seed of ability
Planted in Misery's Field
Where the soil of pain lies fertile
Promising to grow

Crows and ravens scavenge the soil
Underneath gray skies
Even in the rising wind
Threatening to blow

In this field the seeds of life are sown
Flourishing rows of calamity
While rains weep from stormy skies above
Falling down below

462

The distance can only be determined

By the no. 1 tool and the no. 1 new

Hoptollywoggs…

Frogs and fishes

Fiend out in the billious plain

Pain socks me in the head

Pull the curtain Sally

I wish that I was dead!

Caught between that rock and where the hard place starts

Tarts will have you if you don't be careful

Stop wishing for it, Jane!

It will happen!

Sin will have you regardless

Shards of broken glass are a part

Of your journey through this arc of time

Get used to the blood, Billy

Jonathan Lovejoy

Its yours to see!
Blood, billy boy, blood
Cut the skin at the knee
If you don't, you won't make it!

Its cold inside the fish's belly…
Let me out!

463

Someone must have seen the Spirit of Death
And brandished their sharpened sketch pencil
The cloak hides the face of a skeleton
Bony hands carry the scythe in contempt

Death is a loyal companion
Stalking, haunting
Walking among the naïve and the simple
Waiting…

Grieving to swing the sharpened blade

464

Speeding through the land of the dead

Underneath skies of contempt

Those of former privilege are swallowed up

Craving a future among the living

Even while past evils display their colors

On the outskirts of the Great Forest

Instruments of death are hurled through the air

To pierce the heart of the innocent

Pitfalls are found in Swampwood Lane

To carry those of reputation to a pit of suffering

From which no reprieve can be given

No escape from their pain of living

93rd Assembly

465

While moving inside the Halls of Squallor

Pain resounds outside my window

Memories falling in the pouring rain

Drowning joy and happiness

Verses decorate the walls of squallor

Protected from corruption

The grieving gather the verses to themselves

Finding joy and happiness

466

Do you remember what you had to face
When you raced the pace of your favorite race?

The streets were dark
The lights were red
You swore to yourself
That you would soon be dead

When you faced the pace
Of your favorite race

Every intersection bore a sign
To stop before you crossed the line
Before you crashed and bled to death
Before you breathed your dying breath

Do you remember the pace you faced
When you chased the shadows through your favorite race?
Is Destiny going to let you live?
Will Fate let you live another life to give?

Recklessy?

467

High in the blue sky above
In the wispy clouds of summer
Two lights appear in the daytime sky
Shining the color of crimson

Two intrepid points of light
Shining bright red stars
Glowing in the wispy cloud
In the skies of deep blue summer

468

Bring me comfort and peace of mind

Soothe my troubled soul

My aching spirit cries out for thee

For solace in my final hour

Let the Spirit of Death be sent far away from me, O Lord!

Grieve thine heart to be merciful unto me

Send your spirit to my troubled soul

That I may know a day without fear and sorrow…

Or pain

94th Assembly

469

*T*he baby infant spoke to me

Saying "I can see the angel heart"

470

*I*n the grieving land
Under the fall of night
I went to the amaranthine station
To find the berry blue

When I saw the color of berry blue
I grieved the death of Mary Lou

Berries the girth of ripened melons
In the color trail the fairy flew
Lost underneath the fall of night
In the spell of Mary Lou

471

*F*or this reason, a man shall leave his mother and father behind

So that natural tendencies will flow

Wives who promise loyalty

Whose heart is filled with adultery

Whose minds are as corrupted as can be

Broken technology, mad hatters spouting their nonsense

People mill around in the carnival world

Lost souls on the path to Lucipher's Lair

On the way to where souls will cry *never fair* for all eternity

Mulitiplexes of sin and carnality

Holding men and women captive by the millions

Waiting to be entertained, waiting to be shown the right way

Waiting to be rescued

Men must leave their mother's heart

To find the heart of another

To drift among the feminine jungle trees

Where the fruits of their labour will fall

Elizabethan IV

Some will phase into the carnival world
Promising loyalty
Speaking lies
Smiling friendliness in cordiality

Only to flee upon the current of false fear and shame
Into the arms of disloyalty and betrayal

Scattered throughout this world is the demon hoarde
Beings filled with the lust for violence
The desire to do harm
These, avoid like the plague

Keep them at a distance
So that violence may not rule the day
So that peace may be found in the Land of the Walking Dead
Stalking the Land of Dread…

And Death

Talking is instead for those who lack understanding
Listening is the beginning of knowledge and wisdom
Pray that a calling will come
Falling from these skies of contempt

To protect thine heart from misery
And thy soul from despair
Even those whose purpose is vanity
Are in the midst of paradise

Jonathan Lovejoy

95th Assembly

472

The seed of lust grows in the garden of woman

Planted by a sinful heart

Nurtured by repression

Blossomed by the suppression of morality

By the progression of immorality

This flower entices men without understanding

Without wisdom

Sending vines into his nature…

His desire

473

Behold the joke that is poetry…

And laugh

Behold the joke that is life…

And weep

T is for terrific…

Or terrible

474

Above the battlefields of perpetuity
His silhouette was known

Walking tall among the wounded
Providing strength to their dying hour
Giving solace to the discombobulated troops in battle
Reminding them of their calling

The grandest nation on the face of the earth
Threatening to break in two
Until the lean man spoke words of Heaven's Wisdom
The lone figure in the wilderness of battle

Above the battlefields of perpetuity
His silhouette was known

Engaging the spirit of the Lord
He ruled from the House of White
Lost in the power of God
Entranced by the rising tide of wisdom

Elizabethan IV

Here, on this side of paradise
On the other side of sanity
Sacrificing happiness
And his chosen way of life

Drifting as a silhouette of dreams
From one side of blood to the other
Helpless in the flow of time itself
Showing him the way

Growing into a mountain peak
Of knowing what to do
To reverse the pain of a curse
The curse of greed which led to the bloody war

An evil of such power
As to confound all reasoning
All supposition
All attempts to understand

This evil reached out from the time of Appomatox
To touch the hearts and souls of the grandest nation
The curse whose end began in perpetuity
When the man of wisdom ruled in the House of White

Entranced by the rising tide of knowing
Underneath the Power of God
Beneath stormy skies of recompence
And the reward that was due

When clouds of war hath departed

When the pain of vengeance hath gone

The man of lean was burned in the fires of hatred

Taken down in the prime of life

A man whose cause had been that of righteousness

And good will toward men

Now the flag waves over the grandest nation…

Blowing in the Winds of Time

475

Promises made… are not promises kept

Even while sounds threaten to scream into eternity

Phantoms drift from days before

Thriving upon duplicity

Men of means from the land of plenty

Come to the heart of the grieving land

Seeking a new soul to exploit in the evening tide

Looking for another soul to kill

While others are given the power of versatility

The ability to perform

Some struggle in the sea of inadequacy

Pulled away from the shores of success

Being told the truth about their aspirations

That no clear path will be shown

Hope falls to earth like dying leaves

Giving no heed to their crying

Jonathan Lovejoy

Ladders fall clanging to earth

While souls connect in grieving

In the realization of their accursedness

Their wish to have never been born

96th Assembly

476

*G*hosts roam the halls of poverty

Masquerading as human

People whose lives know only the stench of squallor

The sadness of want and need

One who dresses in fine cloth, white button red line down the middle

Above gray wrapped by the black band of torture

Spitting venom from his mouth to those he bore

Who remain sore from his serpent's strike in the noonday

In the turning flow of evening

Another drifts through the halls of squallor

Smiling, oblivious to pain

Pain she craved and nurtured while it grew

Blossoming into a fire of contempt

She wanders through these poverty stricken halls

Waiting to die

Wishing for a reprieve from the life she was given

Trying to break free, but being unable to

Elizabethan IV

Blood flows through the generations like a river
Carrying the curse from the tree of life
A curse bestowed when the banks of the river crumbled
And the tree of death fell into it splashing

Contaminating the flow of life

Who can stem the tide of hatred
That flows through the generations
From father to son
From mother to daughter

Until words are laced with poison
Biting the soul and the spirit
Killing all desire for the future
Where the River of Corruption will flow

477

If you're in America…

Have no regrets

You were born in the greatest country in the world

You became a citizen in the land of plenty

This is the Land of Freedom

The Land of Liberty

Freedom is a place where all men strive to be

Some have died while they sought this glorious homeland

This earthen paradise of prosperity

The Power of God is upon this great nation…

From sea to shining sea

478

Under a deep blue sea

Beneath the ocean that is sky

We turn our gazes high above

To where the dove swims idly by

Flying…

Soaring the heights of our desire

In the ocean that is sky

479

The world can be a dirty place at times
A placed corrupted with evil hearts
Where dens of pain and iniquity grow
Carried by seeds of lust and greed

Lust for power
Lust for glory
The unquenching desire for fame
A place where blue lions roar to adulation

Running to and fro

Some will speak to listening ears
Being central to their fold
Others will bark mighty words of wisdom
Heard by no one

Souls who crave the pain and suffering of the glory seekers
Desiring to torture them until they are broken and weeping
Not understanding that they are doing a fool's bidding
Satisfying their lust for attention

Elizabethan IV

Their groaning instinct for carnality

Honing their public skills all the while
Learning to endure the stoning
The public scorn and ridicule
The tragic death of sincerity

Celebrating the birth of insincerity
The growth of phoniness and idle chatter
Rain clattering from skies of corruption
Spattering the rooftops of their new desire

Their new calling

480

Spirits roam the land of sunset
Underneath clouds of amber light
Eternity grieves the dying day
When Earth turns toward the fall of night

Rising above the earthen shore
Angels survey winter's eve
As nighttime descends their darkest day
Upon the valley of lost souls to grieve

Far beneath the western gate
In the world beyond the evening flow
Bereaving hearts are condemned to wait
For the right hand Power of God to show

481

On a ride beneath the stars of heaven

In a chariot crimson red

Messages send greetings from beyond contempt

In the land where evil serpents play

Crossing over into commerce and industry

Flows a man from the snake land

Who sends greetings from the shores of antipathy

Sitting on a mountain of gold

I ride beneath the stars of heaven

In a chariot of crimson red

Being driven backwards by foolishness

While instinct flashes overhead

Caverns are a threat to living

Growing on either side of the road

Knowing when the road will end

To wait for the chariot crimson red

While I ride the chariot unawares

Beneath the stars of heaven

Jonathan Lovejoy

97th Assembly

482

A scream overcomes the streets of perpetuity
Drawing the dispossessed to the house of birth
Inside rests the scene of his darkest fear
Dripping with life and blood

Death approaches the offspring without reason
Sending torment into days of youth
Suffering betrayal at the hands of trusted friends
Leaving him for dead

483

Remembering times of old
When inspiration flowed like a river
Now farewell falls like winter snow
To bury melody in her tomb

Melody is laid to rest
In the land of forgotten dreams

484

Symbols of marriage lost

Replaced by junk in black tape

While beauty drifts the halls of trade

Seeking assistance

In the palace of earthen divinity

Patrons are captive by the moving colors on the wall

Images seeking a status of importance

In the palace of theology

Looking to revisit Muse's Whisper

Having faded to nothingness

The trade man attempts to escape responsibility

For the anguish he has caused

485

Problems appear in Border
Where danger lurks invisible
Waiting to claim health
From those seeking hospitality

Jonathan Lovejoy

98th Assembly

486

One is the Belle of Amherst

Shy, fearful of the world

A prisoner of verses

Drowned in sweetness too complete to know

She looks through living eyes…

Eyes imagining the world she could never see

Having fear of its inevitable end

Passions unknown and unnurtured

Having love for a father of the world

Crying for a mother's love unrequited

Whose veins flow with the spirit of loving kindness

And fear

This is the face of life

There is another…

The face who hides inside the mirror

This is the Queen of Wicked Verse

Spinning words like a demon

Elizabethan IV

Spitting words of hidden venom and atrocity
Abominations laced in beauty
Corruption hidden in flowers
Lust and lasciviousness...

Perversions beyond depravity
Covered in pulchritudinous prose
This is the evil eye—
The face which understands

The face of unearthly boldness
Gazing a line through cultured civility
Knowing the evil heart beneath the surface of desire
Reflecting it in rhyme

This is the face of hatred and contempt
Given through this gift
The power to see mankind
For the shortcoming that it is

For the disappointment it has always been
For the moral failure it will ever and forever be
This is the Hidden One
Who lives in the shadows of her own creation

Flying witchery through every wall and window
Peering into the wicked heart of every soul
This is the evil eye...
The face of death

487

This was the place where she died

The watermelon girl of Martin County

In the old Moravian church beyond the hill

In the valley by the Durnham Wood

The church sits empty

Void of the life that can be seen

This is the place where she died

On a Sunday morning

Beneath clouds of mourning for what was known

She was taken from her sleeping bed

Made to bathe

Made to dress

Escorted by her grieving mother to the old Moravian church

Where she was to undergo the watermelon call

The punishment for what she had done

The girl of six was called to the front of the congregation

Elizabethan IV

Where she stood in six year old humiliation
To suffer initiation

This was the cleansing punishment they said
For all the things she had done
They split the watermelon in two
In the manner of a murdered head

And they held her down on her back
Where she was scolded and fed

They each placed watermelon into her mouth
Praying...

Jumping...
Calling the name of the Lord
That the watermelon purity would flow through her veins
Until she was free from sin

They held her down through the coughing and chokes
Through every choking and cough that was born
Through every tear that fell
They fed her the watermelon red

Until they saw that sin had fled
Until her body was dead
The quantity flooded her bowels with poison
Until her body was dead

Jonathan Lovejoy

She died because of sin, they said

The mother was held in shrieks and screaming
As her watermelon girl lay dead

Those who live a century away
Look upon the old Moravian Church
Surviving the years of wind and rain
Home to tiny creatures of the Wood

Those who have dared have walked by and bye
To see the church in the fall of night
They claim to have heard a scream to end all screams
And to have seen what no living eyes should see

A tiny figure made of white
Moving around inside
It is the girl who underwent the watermelon call
A century before

488

Salvation never rests in doubt
Along the course of the spirit ride
A ride along the road to Nowhere's Land
Where every dream is forgotten

Foolishness comes in irresistible stone
The blue of every sky and ocean
With the ivory of salt
And sugar crystal forms

When these stones are placed together
They glow with the music of alien light
A sight foreign to those on the spirit ride…
It is the light of joy and hope

489

To drift upon its icy air

Noontime refusals

Wishing a reprieve from noise

When games are played

Old desires

New jealousies

Twisted psychologies reign

Chiming the noontime train

99th Assembly

490

The wayward child was given a choice
By the mother who was a kindly sort

A striping with the electric chord
A burning with the iron
A paddling with the board…
Until bruises turn to blood

If it weren't for me, the mother cried
You wouldn't be like this anymore
You wouldn't act as though you deserved
To be whipped with the electric chord

But the child could not endure the board
Nor the fire from the chord
Nor the heat in the middle of his back
As the iron's just reward

So the wayward child chose the dark'ned cupboard
Where the grapes of wrath are stored…
He cried while she locked him in the cupboard
Where the wrath of woman is stored

491

September 11, 2001

COMPLACENCY reigned supreme
On the day the towers fell
One thousand feet of concrete, glass and steel
Broken into pieces

Turned into a shower of dust
When flaming arrows are flown from the east—
Burning blue and black fire
Arrows of scorn, contempt and hatred

Men despising their bretheren
Unable to live in a world of peace and harmony
Where happiness is king
But complacency reigns supreme…

On the day the towers fell

Jonathan Lovejoy

September 11, 1991

Voices crying from GRAVES across the ocean
CRYING FOR A REPRIEVE from bondage
Crying for vengeance
For the shedding of their innocent blood

These are voices of mothers and fathers
Sons and daughters
Whole FAMILIES KILLED AND BURIED
In the days before the towers fell

But vengeance flows the River of Time
Until its blessed day is come
THEIR REPRIEVE—FLOWN UPON ARROWS OF CONTEMPT
Flung—at the towers of glass and steel
In the land where COMPLACENCY reigns supreme

VENGEANCE IS MINE, SAITH THE LORD
On the day the towers fell

492

Yellow and silver color the night breeze

Above the sea of battle

Faces hypnotized in combat

Waiting to die

493

Above the eastern horizon
In the sky beyond the hill
The full moon rises in the evening day
Painted the color of blood

Climbing to the top of the hill
To gaze across the land of grieving
Selene bears the color of rust
For the last generation

494

Destiny appears outside my door

Seeking whom it may devour

Hearkening from unknown days before

Grieving for my final hour

A dark destiny appears outside my door

Lurking devastation and power

Jonathan Lovejoy

100th Assembly

495

O Little Town…

Across the desert sea

Flowing… above the mountains of the East
Rests a light shining in glory
A light seen in both day and night
Shining above the promise of God

Lighting the path to Redemption
Showing the way to a reprieve from a curse
Given from the Garden of Eden

O Little Town…
Across the desert sea

Where the promise of God rests in a stable
Shining above winter's eve
This is a light to guide all souls
Through the Valley of the Shadow of Death

Elizabethan IV

Beyond this valley is a promise
Bestowed from ages before the Fall
The promise is wrapped in swaddling clothes…
Lying in a manger

O Little Town…
Across the desert sea

High above the sand infinity
The star shines both day and night
So every eye shall see Him

Across the night's infinity
On the trail of winter's eve
The Mercy of God will reign supreme
When the star fades from the sky

Its light will shine for an eternity…
Above the hearts of men
Guiding them through the valley
To the shores of the Promised Land

O Little Town…
Across the desert sea

Shepherds and Magi still roam and wander
Looking for the Star to guide them…

Across the desert sea

496

Love in the name of discipline
A bludgeoning fisted glove
Caught by the whirling leather strap
Disciplined by the Love…

And then the pounding of her contempt
And the breaking of the board
Punished by the preacher's robe…
In the name of our precious Lord

497

She answers the fateful knocking

He's a pig, she thinks

She's a cow, he thinks

Little calves and piglets galore

In wedded bliss

498

The line starts at the center

Passing through the heart

Then it winds outward…

Into space nearby

Turning upward, the line joins the third dimension

Drawing power from the air around the body

It begins to rise upward rapidly

Curving rightward

The line turns an eternal curve,

To never meet itself

To never return to the source…

The path it leaves burns energy in a circle

Where energy is born and lives

Never dying in the lifetime of the source

Its place of birth

Elizabethan IV

From the living room, I feel the line giving birth to itself
Passing through the heart, into the space to my left
Curving upward to its destiny…
A perpetual right

Turning
Curving…
Sweeping past itself
Feeding upon the energy of its own Creation

Pushed along by the unseen
Rising through the ceiling
Crossing through the attic, and downward
Circling back below

Diving into the earth beneath
Past the grave of the unknown carcass
The bones of a beast or being
Continuing the trip downward and around

Climbing up through the floor farther away
Slicing through the ceiling farther away
Climbing higher
Higher this time

Bursting through the roof of my poverty home
Out into the nighttime drizzle
The whizzle of fizzling rain dying in a twizzle

Slicing through every drop in unseen, invisible blue
Arching rightward, falling
Falling…
Down to the darkened grass underneath

Underneath its trajectory
Away from the house
Plunging through soil undisturbed
Undeterred

Rounding out its journey below once again
Curving down and far below the ground
Speeding into rising
Climbing…

Flowing…
A smooth growing toward the night rain
Bursting through in energy unseen once again
Many blocks from the house of poverty's reign and rule

Climbing into its circle
High above every tree…
Turning itself in perfection
Afar off,

Elizabethan IV

High over where the roof of its birth lay in drowning
In grieving,
Gathering momentum,
Upon this plunge through time, rippling outward

Falling blocks away
In the midst of the forest grove of trees
Plowing beyond where any graves were ever dug and laid
Deeper than plans best having never been made to lay

Turning through the cold and dark beneath again
Looping upward
Bursting through the soil of a far away field
Beyond the lights of the city

Riding high in the Winter Rain
To where clouds stretch to earthen infinity

Every journey appears as a line of concentrus
Paths having no beginning or end
Without common origin
But they are born at a single point in space

Moving unbroken through the hours
The days
The years
Appearing as rings

As circles plural

But being only one line of thought…

Unbroken

499

Eyes can be many things

They can indeed be windows to the soul

Or they can be a fortress of solitude

A barrier

Eyes of pure understanding

Greely eyes

Eyes with wisdom and knowledge from beyond the grave

Not from the heavenly place

Watching humanity

Every hour of the day, every second of every hour

Eyes of pure understanding

Greely eyes

To see them is to see a cause for flight

Though you will be held immobile by their power

Looking human, having no unearthly appearance

But possessing otherworldly comprehension

Stare not into the eyes of knowledge

The face of wisdom

A face appearing to have courtesy

But being only malice...

With evil intention

SATAN stares through these eyes...

Eyes of pure understanding

500

The evidence of promises kept

Leapt onto her back

Until she wept…

Then slept in blood and pain

Jonathan Lovejoy

101st Assembly

501

*Y*oung holds commodities in compassion
Old seeks to dismiss

Exteriors of salt and brine

Corrupted by sugar

Friends come and go

Relatives in the poverty house

All adrift in a dust wind

Rust accumulated

502

Verses are hidden from the wise

Revealed to the simple

Along a sandy shore

In a village by the sea

Destiny drowns a life in turmoil

In a village by the sea

503

Green and Gold harbor corruption

Hidden in prosperity

Black covers a life in turmoil

Exploding clouds of the apocalyptic

In vexation the clouds are drawn

The seed of devastation

Personalities bark through smiles of indifference

Drawing inferiority from their worshippers

Melodies ask to be sung!

Longing to be set free!

Whispers of death in ice

Permeate the soul

Mocking a life buried in pain

Entombed in frustration

HELL is filled to capacity

When the passenger plane explodes in the sky

Kissed by another in a ball of fire

Flaming toward the sea

504

Melody sounds the moving train

Speeding from obscurity

Calling from the wilderness

Deep inside the woods

The train gathers momentum

Rolling through the Appalachian Forest

To wreak havoc on a dying world

To perish in a great noise

To explode in a revelation

Confounding dead sensibilities

The train speeds toward the wall of resistance

Irrepressibly

Jonathan Lovejoy

102nd Assembly

505

Hope drips ineffectively

Ticking with the clock

Marking destiny in time

With every second that will be

Predetermined life

Plans made before birth

The stirring of every breeze…

Every breath

506

From the mouth of man
Serpents crawl invisible
Biting helpless souls nearby
Filling them with poison

Crippled spirits
Wounded psychologies
Every insult is pain inflicted
Invisibly

507

The bloody Hilaried

Killed by pain from Eastern Wood

In the million dollar home

Of a Free Man

508

The sister did the deed

The fire kept the belle in the dark

Hiding her in smoke

From Amherst

Jonathan Lovejoy

103rd Assembly

509

O, to see a sunrise unhindered

Uncluttered by urban sprawl

The blight of buildings

Half dead trees

Oh, to see a sunrise over the prairie

Where the land is unburdened by bricks and glass

My heart rises above the clamour

Where I can see the sunrise over the prairie

When I see daybreak above the city

I can feel the rising sun

510

This city is a blight
I've walked along these lonely, dark
And dirty streets all night

You may very well be right
But your plight will likely not improve
In the early morning light

511

Fear glides icy roads

Before Winter's Gloaming

Carrying disillusionment

On a passenger ride

The road stretches toward evening

Treacherous

Pain entombed by ice and snow

Beckoning them

512

I walked with the man of music
Under skies of ashen gray regret

Braving the rising storm of ridicule
Past the houses of despair and abject poverty
Souls that should have never been born look on
Wallowing in disillusionment

Waiting to see the man of music
Crushed in the weight of duplicity
Ground to pieces in a blade of lies
Killed by the sword of envy

The dagger of jealousy

I walked with the man of music
On the streets of the Grieving Land

As trouble in every kind and color wash before us
Among problems lay the colors of a former life
We attempt to gather remnants of joy and civility
In vain

Jonathan Lovejoy

Strolling through the Grieving Land
In the company of the man of music
Past the buildings that rise into the sky
Threatening to fall

Into the hall of ambiguity we drift
Into the Moving Room
The moving room proves to be easily as a tomb
Masquerading as assistance

The room loses itself in the flow of time
Revealing nothing of its progression
Ticking away the hours like minutes
Then the minutes like hours

In the company of the Music Man
I emerge from the tomb
Into a world raining ashes of scorn and mocking
Superheating the air

Burning cinders of derision
Threatening to burn the land into smoke and soot
Through the aftermath of lies
We stroll the landscape of demons and devastation

Elizabethan IV

Breathing the superheated air
In a world obliterated by false witness
By the craving of lustful envy
With demonic covetousness

And jealousy

In the world of ashen gray regret
I stroll along with the man of music
Whose eyes bear the burden of genius...

And fear

513

In the game of life and death

The truck won the prize

Those in the car were killed…

Instantly

Blood and twisted metal

Broken glass

Bodies without souls

Paradise or Hell

104th Assembly

Jonathan Lovejoy

514

Divorce looms the couple's future
Like a serpent from the Garden of Eve
A curse bestowed from antiquity
Hidden in the bloodline

Women of Beauty bring misery to the earth
Disguised as harmless diversion
Infidelity appears in serpentine
Stealthily

In the chapel, the couple sits in bitterness
While the world drowns in a sea of foolishness
A woman with short dark hair haunts them
Mockingly

Freedom calls from North beyond ninety five
Creating instability
While offspring in the bliss of ignorance
Choose to follow their heart

Elizabethan IV

The serpent strikes their loving spirit

Permeating poison throughout

Now, the loving spirit struggles to breathe life

Desperately

515

Life is not a graveyard

So try hard not to weep

When the pain of living is cold and deep...

Pray the Lord your soul to keep

516

Humankind places conditions on love
Love which they give reluctantly

Beyond filth and corruption
There is no lying tongue
No false witness against a fellow citizen
No gatherings held in secret

Conspiracies…

Plans to infuse another's life with poison
To kill their reputation
Women heavy laden with sins
Men burdened by the sorrow of abomination

Violence does not exist alone
It is an act perpetrated by nature
The clouds…
The sea

The earth itself
And every inhabitant therein

There are those who conspire in secret
Whispering devastation
Hissing destruction on their fellow citizen
To bring him to ruin

When they are confronted
Asked why this monstrosity
Why this atrocious atrocity
The response is inevitably the same

Shrugged shoulders
Pointed fingers
Raised eyebrows
All hiding the lack of honesty

The sin of cruelty to their fellow man
Like a pack of wolves
Turning on the weakest among them
To tear them to pieces

Instinctively

517

The lady chauffeur passed the test
To prove her worthiness for a duty
She drove me on a ride to rest
Displaying kindness with her beauty

518

Although their time had been forbidden

The wife had been untrue

Now, she was no longer hidden

From a comeuppance overdue

519

Trapped inside a burning room
The prisoner wanted out
He died inside a fiery tomb
'Til his ashes blew about

Fancy Comfort mourned the death
Of Jasper Hennesey
Beside her mother Lula Beth
In backwoods Tennessee

While Lula kept their love forbidden
Jasper had been untrue
Now Death lurked where Recompense lay hidden
Their comeuppance that was due

Fancy roped her mother bound
Tight from head to foot
While splashing kerosene around
To burn their cabin to soot

Jonathan Lovejoy

Trapped inside a burning room
The prisoners wanted out
They died inside a fiery tomb
'Til their ashes blew about

520

Everything is as clear as the wind

That is why fate allows us to see through the window

What do we see?

Death

The quality of mercy is not strained, he said

It rains upon the just...

And the unjust

Jonathan Lovejoy

105th Assembly

521

*T*he glory of the Lord is freedom (the Chorus of the Slaves)

The nation never warmed to our greeting
To our beating heart
So we had to reach through time and history
For the reward that was due

Even while the swords of battle clamoured through cold wintry knights
Even when fireballs boomed from the cannons of war
Even while heat rained down from the rifles and pistols
Upon the bodies of every dedicated soldier in battle

We knew that what we were promised
Would not be given by willing hands
Or would not be a prize easily won
Somehow we knew, even while tears of mighty realization began to flow

That the promise of freedom
Would be in a place far away from where we stood
And the journey would be long
And our suffering would be great

And that the Glory of the Lord would choose to shine upon us
In its own appointed time
In its own appointed day
Even in its own appointed hour

We knew that someday
We would be able to lift our eyes
Towards the mighty shores of heaven
And sing praises of thanksgiving to the Almighty God

That this day
This hour
This moment of freedom has come
And that God has at last revealed his love to us

Along the Shores of this great nation
Through the forests, over the mountains
Over every hill and valley…
The Glory of the Lord has shown

522

I saw a nuclear blast outside my window
It was 50 miles away
The fire cloud played a mushroom crescendo
In the evening of my final day

523

I see the moon in a daytime sky

Surrounded by burning red leaves

Through a circle in the fire tree

The moon shines its last day

Yellow blonded beauties

Adrift in narcissism

Hear nothing of the truth

On their way out the door

The Tree of Eschatology grows steadily in spring

Branches in a perfect circle around a hole

Through which the end time can be seen

In a daytime sky

As distance gathers between logic and the tree

The circle vanishes in a mass of red leaves—

Shrinking away

Then the tree joins every other condemned earth tree

In the song of autumn

Jonathan Lovejoy

The landscape is a winter forest
Of spring trees in waiting
Trees which will wait this time
For an eternity

While the Tree of Eschatology grows
Demons flow in from perpetuity
Bringing past woes—refusing to vanish away
Mocking the soul

Through the branches of the fire tree
The end time rules the sky
Relying on the flow of time
And history

524

Luxury calls from a distant place
Tormenting two souls in poverty
Filling them with false hope and dreams
Of a better life

Snow falls to their longing
To cover a trail in winter white
Until their dreams are buried...
In the frozen earth

525

*I*n the Library of Common Lore

Seeds of grief are clearly sown

As the sacred scrolls are mocked by the ill informed

Their words are gathered together

Among the wood burnished to perpetuity

Angels protect the scrolls from scorn

In the final days of preparation

The blood of the scribe is shed to completion

Where the woman of music is born

Angels of the Lord are sent from the four winds

Each to carry a section of the Heavenly Parchment

In the manner of a sacred book

The scribe moves under the weight of mocking

Through the Halls of Lore and Learning

Carrying a portion of the scrolls

A section of the book

Elizabethan IV

Knowing nothing of how it is assembled

Following the angel's divine decree

A book formed in the Winds of Time

And eternity

Jonathan Lovejoy

106th Assembly

526

Divorced Mom After Burying Her Five Year Old Daughter

(Fish and Ham in the Kitchen)

MELODY sings its praises
To what!
You better go back to the well
Where you belong

Another day on the roller coaster
Won't do any good
She's still the lion
Grassy!

Sassy!
Brassy with the biscuits
Honey tastes sweet
When its poured over the bread

Call the coroner, Sally
I wish that I was dead!
Wishes
Dishes

Elizabethan IV

Fishes
What mishmash is this?
Left to rot in the Woods
Your corpse is due

Cut to the chase, baby
Your comeuppance is overdue!

You're not going to escape it
So don't waste time trying to fake it
Balloons are like jelly
In the poisoned air

Hairspray is in the delly
When the Briar Strone is in the chair
Pick it up!
Feel it up!

Lick it up, Momma!
Its calling your payment due
Cook the ham and slam the bird

Your pies are burning…

Jonathan Lovejoy

527

The Teenage Girl Will Loose her Virginity
(On Prom Night)

ASK hotbread…
He'll tell you!
Wait for it!
Your heat is on the way

Kiss the honey goodbye, boys
The hotbrand is here to stay!

The sky is turning red, Fred
Blood is raining down
The rivers look like rust, clown
Can't you see it?

This is why it won't happen for you
You won't listen!
The mountains are screaming it at your pills
Take them and get better!

Elizabethan IV

No need to pay the bills, John
The hills are cracking down
Earthquakes and milkshakes
Brian's on the phone!

Speaking to lust and miked out dusting
Sweetie, don't listen to him!
He wants to take your soul
His kind of love you don't need!

528

Aspen On the Eve of Nuclear War

(Ski Bunny's Folly)

STOP sliding down the mountain

Like a foolish boat

Goats have more sense

Than the white iced lasic

Its basic math, you boon

Its going to happen sooner than you think

Explosions in motion

Lotion factories burning

Rivers spreading outward

Drowning grass in the can

The plan is simple…

Run!

Elizabethan IV

You can't have any fun, son

When the Sun comes to get you

If the demons let you live

To see it happen

529

A mountain rolls over the horizon

White glory rising

A cloude lifting towards the sky

Touching the earth

Birds turn away in fear

From the mountain range in the sky

Moving from west to east

Below a double shade of blue

530

*T*eenage Athlete Arrested for Date Rape

(Thunderstorm Over the Jailhouse)

JASON whacked me on the toes

Haytion whacked down on the pros

Creations backed the crown in repose

Crustaceans packed in town

Against those actions you didn't want

But it happened anyway,

Even though she didn't want you to

Put it in the closet, Boy!

Its over!

Balls...

You've got em!

It calls for something else, Paul

Wake up!

Jonathan Lovejoy

Can't you hear the call?
The ground is screaming at you,
But you won't stop to hear it
Thunder from the center…

Feel it, don't steal it!
It heals the body if you conceal it
It don't pay to peel the peppers
They're half the hazard if you reveal it!

531

Love Night for a Suburban Rapist

(A Trip to the Drugstore)

SO…
You think you're ready—
To be blown up with the rest of the world
No…

You're not!

By bye baby bunting
Daddy's gone a hunting
To buy a little lammie skin
To keep it all from going in

Again!

Jonathan Lovejoy

107th Assembly

532

A Five Year Old Curses His Father
(Mother's Words On Friday Night)

BABY FACED and big lipped
The monster said to me
"Son of a bitch," the baby quipped
For all the world to see

The Incredible Hulk played on TV
Grandpa rose from the grave
Catch that spider with a chick pea
And send him to a cave!

533

*Y*oung Couple Burning to Death
(Night Trip off an Ocean Highway)

I DON'T UNDERSTAND

Why you're so angry

The world had to end anyway

Accept it!

He leapt it! You slept it!

She clept it!

In the Immaculate Way…

He recepted it!

The sky is still burning from it

Our skin can't take it!

Our bodies won't make it

The graves won't be big enough to hold us all

So have a piece of Bundt Cake and fake it!

What? You don't understand where this comes from?
Where sin comes out?
Don't fret about it Gertrude…
This dude is whacked!

He burst the sack
In Wheaterzine
Greet her when you see her
She's in the same place you're going, Joe!

More fire, don't you know!

II

*W*oman Cheating on Her Parapalegic Husband
(Rendezvous in a Mountain Cabin)

THE WORLD IS A MESS
Say it don't spray it!
Respect the TV actress
Hold your scorn for the Movie Queen!

Quiet, you whispering Willies!
Beauty's on the scene
She's doing her duty on the mean
Her jeans are on fire

Elizabethan IV

Red hot in a Swack Backed cabin
Doing the nasty dance!
She's in the middle of the woods
Nobody's there to hear it

We cheer it!
Don't sneer it!
Don't jeer it!
Don't go near it!

Can't you hear it, boy?
Its calling you
Even the trees said
Go to it!

Get on your knees and pray to Sam in the Hills
That you do it
If you go, you're dead
You'll flake into a stone

Your life's at stake here, Johnny Boy
Shut up and go back home!

You've been warned, Kenny
Cathy's on the prowl
The growl you hear coming out of the woods...
Its for you!

534

Confessions of a Female Murder Victim

(The Corpse in the Basement)

I DON'T KNOW why she's so angry
The reason the rocks fell from the sky
Was because of her sin,
Not mine

Whoops!
Maybe it was mine, Simpkin

Be a dolly dimkin for me, Wilkin
Frip filly filkin
When the Alabasters whipped the snails!

Gee Whiz, Al!
What are we saying…
Nothing!

Elizabethan IV

If this is what HELL is like
Then every demon here can kiss my
Acabaca
My soda cracka

My GTO
By booty…hold it!

Did Momma cut the cat out of the bag this Spring?
I don't know…
But the world is gone—
Because of something she did

Apples!
Oranges!
Fruit from the Tree
The serpent said it best, son

Get the mail!

Perfle's head is resting
In the cooler in the basement
That cat jumped out of the bag
And ran away after it happened…

He saw me die!

II

*W*idow on the Verge of Suicide

(Pills and a Glass of Wine)

ITS SOMETHING BETTER

Than we ever pieced for a new world

There's no need to try…

Crying won't help the forest grow—

Dry your eyes!

Read the lying book

Snookery is the way of things here, girl

Get used to it!

He ain't coming back to Houston Street

So why don't you go ahead and booze it

Loose it if you want…

It doesn't matter!

Eat as much as you want…

Get fatter!

Rocks play games when you aren't looking

They play GUESS THE SIN

They look into the lives of idiots

And make fun

Elizabethan IV

You're not always going to have confidence
So be careful
Don't insist on resisting the fear
When the clouds turn red

When blood rains down
You'll be dead

Don't fret it, don't sweat it
Just look inside your head
You know Armageddon is coming
So pack a pair of shoes

Walk away from it sister
Your life is down the tubes!

535

*D*ive off a Mountain Bridge in Winter

(The Dead Fool in the River)

GO!

Play with your friends while you can

Its almost done here

Horse riders jumped the Canyon Trail

In the poisoned snow

Go on…

Eat a cone!

Die well while you can

You may as well check out of it now

How'd you ever get born?

108th Assembly

536

To be a poet is a curse

While melody is king

Only a fool would write a verse

For any bird to sing

Profound meaning, for some

For others—

Profoundly meaningless

This is the music of Life…

Of Poetry

537

Verses are the music man's delight

When gray envelops the sky

HELL is the devil's domain

While they prepare for the journey

538

I once looked in the mirror

And thought I saw beauty

I knew quickly that it was Illusion

A trick of the mind

My own image…

Came back inside the mirror

539

Pick a place and go THERE

Then stay there all alone

If there are no people

Then call that place your own

THERE are no guarantees in life

Disaster is like a dome

Every soul is filled with strife

There is no happy home

540

*I*n the Wilderness of Lost Hope

Ghosts whisper "Were you ever there?"

In sorrow they endeavor to cope

Two souls adrift—Never Fair

541

The pastor was a kindly sort

Who had a perfect life

They sentenced him to death in court

For murdering his wife

542

The candy chocolates are being eaten

The flowers are in the trash

The wayward kids are being beaten

With the buckle of the lash

109th Assembly

543

"I'm sick to death of this poverty," she said
"I can't live here any more"
But her mother only shook her head
Having heard it all before

"Being poor is good," she said
"It's what God called us for"
But her daughter merely shook her head
And went quietly out the door

544

The bus is here

It's time to go

But circumstances won't adhere…

Don't you know

One is sick

In a dying bed

The other's mind won't click…

Its dead

545

Heroes conquer dreary days
Along the forest trail
Invulnerability flies in color
Above the cruel and the simple

Disillusionment finds a calling
Among the predetermined elite
Where expected derision falls ineffective
Along the forest trail

546

"Let me see your grades," the mother said
To see what is below an A
He handed his mother the card in dread
Knowing what price he would pay

With a twinkle in her lovely eye
She noticed a C and a D
Her son had already begun to cry
Knowing what his punishment would be

The mother said, "This isn't good"
"Take off your pants and wait here for me"
She returned with a piece of paddling wood
And took her son over her knee

She beat him 'til his skin was raw
In the haze of a slow motion dream
Her legs were the only things he saw
Through tears and a piercing scream

547

While seeking a new way to go

The angel renders a possibility

Providing no strength for me to know

This exercise in futility

548

$\mathcal{B}$EWARE the fireplace troll

He appears to little girls in their dreams

Mezmerizing them

Whispering lies

Smiling

The fireplace troll appears in many forms

All variant of the theme…

Deceit

549

I read the Word of the Lord

And I tremble

Every word is Power and Truth

I cannot look upon thy face!

It burns my soul in a fire

Its beauty is a flame to my eyesight

It giveth agony to my wayward heart

It is acid to my wicked soul

The fool saith in his heart "There is no God"

The Lord is revealed in every Word of Scripture

Every heart crieth for redemption

And every soul for a reprieve!

550

ON BOARD the Train to Nowhere

Soldiers wait in grieving

While the disillusioned repairs a life in turmoil

Helping others on the train

While the train rolls intrepidly along

An angel offers help to the despised

All underneath skies of contempt

Threatening a mighty rain

The train moves with the current of time

Carrying passengers from birth to death

A sanctuary for the blessed and the unblessed

Rolling steadily along

Jonathan Lovejoy

110th Assembly

Jonathan Lovejoy

551

*F*ire on the Beach (Put Your Clothes On, Honey!)

Curvaceousness beckons through immodesty
Calling forth lust
Confounding the wise and the simple
To burden the heart with instinct

As the hungry tiger prowls the forest
So to does the soul of a man
Beckoned by Immodesty's Flame
Until he is consumed

552

The Farmer's Widow

WINDS above the ocean of green
To where the Lady stands bereaving
Teardrops touch a face in grieving
Kisses from the farmer's rain

553

Perversions live among humanity

Seeking a vessel to coincide

From lasciviousness to vanity

A heart in which to hide

554

In the company of the music man
Struggling to hold his attention
I craft verses as best I can
Too inadequately to mention

The music man spoke to me
In good natured ridicule
Watching my opportunity choke for me
In the chamber of where the critics rule

The barber takes his place nearby
Removing a dweeby two-way hat
While the music man gets the weary blear-eye
Like a sleepy cat on a cashmere mat

A dead chance is buried on the Hill
In the company of the music man
Desperate for the Barber of Seville
In days before One with an Anti-Christ plan

111th Assembly

555

O Heavenly Father
Thy blessings to send
In thunder and rain
And rising wind

Shine thy face
Upon the harvest yield
Descend thy Grace
Upon this Harvest Field

556

Someone Once Called In A Lie

on this poor chap

Putting Him Off Being In A
public place, this poor sap

557

Demons from the past appear

Drowning in contempt

Reenergized by self loathing

In a new facility

The demon harbors secret hatred

Under a cloak of civility

Despising every soul he knows…

From a smile of gentility

558

Encounters over a half a century
And two decades long ago
Don't mean a thing to my withering corpse
Entombed in the ground below!

The grass is gone in the arctic breeze
In the field of winter's white
Be wary of your stepping, if you please
The ground here is frozen with spite!

559

The power of God is mighty indeed

The smallest part of it

Is greater than all mankind

He shall reveal himself in clouds of mercy

And judgment

112th Assembly

Jonathan Lovejoy

560

When I close my eyes I see

A lady in a white coffin

Rolling around the ridge of a precipice…

Above a grassy hill

The White Chariot takes a tumble

To become a cloud of glass and noise

And crumpling metallic sound

At the bottom of the hill

The woman is lost inside the cloud

Inside the white coffin

Waiting to be buried

Her eyes are open…

Her blood is red

When I close my eyes I see

The lady in the white coffin

Lowering beneath the ground

Underneath the dirt and the New Rain

Elizabethan IV

Her white chariot awaits

To whisk her away to a new journey

To a place beyond where my eyes can see

561

Mrs. Deaks has all the money, Honey
You couldn't follow her if you tried
So be a butterfly to your children
Shake off that useless pride

The woman with the gray purse is here, Bunny
Her money is bigger than you!
She's going to teach you a thing or two
About what's doing in the Well-to-Do!

562

Rescue me from the bands of poverty
Constricting me like a serpent
Save me from Death in crimson red
From eyes the color of Serpentine

Undo this spell, you witches!
Unclaw thy wicked hand from my flesh!

563

Still cursed with Poverty and Death
In the days after the dark road
Carrying the passes
Hoping to avoid the Witch Window

Necromancers tell the tale
That a trip through this window is a good thing
Increasing sorrow
Upon the journey toward the grave

Magnifying fear

Those that go through the window risk death
A fall from a great height
Survivors do so in another form
As a ghost in flesh and blood

Having no knowledge that they have died
And that their passes are corrupted
The old passes undergo a cleansing
Before they wither and die away

Elizabethan IV

Worldliness has drawing power
Whispering of the Window
Encouraging the heart
To buy the White Pass

And listen to the witches
Saying "your life can never be complete…"
"Unless you climb through the Window"

564

Every night I die

To wake!

Lest I die again

To sleep is good

Tis no mortal sin

To die and die again

113th Assembly

565

Find Your Own Voice, Poet!

It came from behind the clouds with fervor
Saying, Don't be like her...

Be yourself!
Your voice is stronger
You'll be on the shelf before you know it, girl
The elf has already forseen it!

Pull the bow back
And shoot the sky
Don't look for the arrow
Its gon' fly way too high

You won't be able to see it
It fell into the sea!

She's not for you, poet!
Don't try to imitate her
You can't!
You're making a fool of yourself!

Elizabethan IV

She's for the lonely non-poet
Not you!

566

The Aquarium

Beauty swims in choking death
In the Ocean of Lost Dreams
While pain destroys the dispossessed
In the grieving bed

One thousand feet of hope
Is clipped by incompetence
In the disconcented waters
Of Mirage Lake

567

The Cheerleader

A lot of it has to be
The pleasure derived from pervertedness
Look up and there it is…
Uncovered!

If you want good times
You must have bad times along the way
A walk along the dark road
Too scared to act

Best of luck finding it
It is elusive
Its already clear that you gave up
The headache said so!

568

Weariness in the field of snow

In search of a hiding place to know

With a detour to the learning hall

Where dreariness yearns the Failure's Call

The demon said, you failed the test

Have no shame when you join the rest

Your quest lies in a dying seed

The ruins of an unrequited need

In disillusionment and gloom

Searching through every barren room

It lies beyond what is easy to know

On a journey across the field of snow

114th Assembly

569

The New World Messiah

The American Jesus is a postcard

A calender

A painting

A statue

He has very little meaning beyond these

Except to those entombed by religion

The rest of us are prisoners to skepticism

Ridicule and non-belief

The real Jesus is perhaps what it says

In the Bible

The Son of the Living God

The Redeemer

The Way

The Truth

And the Life

Elizabethan IV

The New American Jesus has been immortalized

For all the world to see

He is the One who shed innocent blood

For our transgressions

570

Dreary days conquer heroes
Trail the forest along
Color flies invulnerability
Simple and cruel above

Calling finds disillusionment
Elite predetermined among
Ineffective falls derision expected
Trail the forest along

571

In the dead land market
Satan's hoarde runs to and fro
Confounding the wise and the simple
In the prolonged spirit of fear

Gathering new patients in a line
Those looking for success in stupidity
Impressing others in the dead land market
Souls beyond the grave

More twists than a cork screw
On a trip through these isles
Savoring the lips of pleasure
The million dollar woman

572

In the Dead Land Market Inn
Fro and to runs Hoarde Satan
Simple and the wise confounding
Spirit of Fear prolonged in

Line in patients gathering new
Stupidity in success for looking those
Market Land Dead in others impressing
Grave beyond the souls

Screw cork than a twist more
Isles these through a trip on
Pleasure of lips the savoring
Woman dollar million

115th Assembly

Jonathan Lovejoy

573

On the Prairie of Death

The corrupt gather to mourn

While innocence seeks a place among them

To pay respects to the dead

574

The Media Man died an early death
He was only 53
No one cried an undesigning breath
For his glamorous debauchery

Sorrow touched his lonely crew
While the Hoarde was rigid and brave
The sky bore the richest Azurean Blue
The sun burned hot over his grave

He woke up in a burning Hell
Clawed by agonizing desire
Knowing why it was his place to dwell
By the sea of brimstone and rolling fire

575

Rest from the weariness…

Rest from your life

Have time off from suffering

From torment…

From the aching spirit

The burning flesh

Rest warmly in the cold ground

Beneath the earth

576

A field of twisters on the open plain

Looking for souls to kill

Confined to where no houses are built

On the prairie field

Trapped in the field of twisters

An invisible one whirls me to infinity

Leaving my body on the ground

Alive so I can see

I look up into the sky

Where the invisible funnel appears

A cloud from the ground to the heavens

Twirling by my head

Hissing and whirling

Kissing the ground

Looking for a soul to kill

577

The Expansion of Humanity

Man is nothing without God
His achievments are meaningless
His accomplishments without merit
All his success is corruption in and of itself

Mankind is capable of natural affection
Powerful niceness
Cordiality mistaken for righteousness
Kindness mistaken for Godliness

But mankind is nothing without God
A race of cold, dead souls
Like demon manifestations
Smiling at each other…

Congratulating
Patting each other on the back
Achieving monumental miracles
In every generation

Elizabethan IV

Even so far as leaving the Earth itself
To take an empty trip among the stars
Wishing to take the Hellish journey
The claustrophobic one way trip

To some cold…
Dead…
Barren…
Lifeless world

In the name of humanity

In places where giant rocks hurl into one another
Common Place
And sand is the ocean
And endless slabs of stone are the shore

Places known and unknown
All in the name of human achievement
Advancement
Sharing niceness with one another

Gladness

With souls as cold and dead…
As the barren worlds they are in

116th Assembly

578

Emily had a Garden View

From the window of a beautiful home

Not a claustrophobic prison

Without fresh air to breathe

If the walls closed in around her

She took a stroll through the Flower Garden

Where honeybees buzzed

Birds chirped a song

And butterflies fluttered

In the breeze

579

I hear the night man coming hence
To show the way to my sleep again
From birth to night until now and since
The deep I fear to be lying in

Into the chariot—away we go!
Along the path to infinity
With no respector of persons to know
He drove our horses to eternity

Through the nighttime grove to beyond the hill
We arrove the Palace of the Rising Mound
Creation breathed while we stood still
At the door of the horizontal resting ground

Now, upon this Advent winter's eve
The Night Man calls a name to fore
With mercy for this new soul to grieve
On the chariot ride to a peaceful shore

580

Clouds of want

Clouds of need

A heavy rainfall

A harvest of greed

117th Assembly

581

A demon lives in the other room
Sitting on the door resting
A notorious blue demon
Eyes in yellow ashe

Roses in this
Arranged in their upright glass coffin
The roses turn to clinking ceramic—
Before my eyes

A blue demon lives in every home
A ghost appeared in flesh and blood
Causing strife

582

The Rituals of Correction

There are those who like to channel—
Their frustrations into their teenagers

A cross word here
A slap there
An angry look here
An insult there

"You stupid teens"
Is the refrain they use
Singing the misery of their life into the air…
And into their children's soul

A song carried through body language
Through words
Through actions
Endless groundings

An infinity of minor infractions…
Acted upon
Chipping away slowly—
At the growing child's self worth

The ultimate is the desire to inflict physical pain
Pain born from the frustrations of life
The pressures of their own living
"You Stupid Teens" becomes a sworn promise, then

A song of revenge
A promise of future punishment in leather
Or wood
Or bare hands across humiliated flesh…

Torture administered
To alleviate their own pain—
In the name of Discipline

Some of these rituals are private
Between the parent and the son
Between the parent and the daughter
But some are carried out in solemn ritual

With other adults invited to watch
To compound the daughter's humiliation
The devastation of her self worth
Or that of the son

These are the Rituals of Correction
The punishments delivered from pervertedness…
From depravity

583

Flaming like a cook upon the lawn
This mournful spirit is shown
To fill my soul with a weeping flood—
Beyond the break of dawn

In the cool of the turning evening day
Smoke arose from the grill
They all said, you're not allowed to stay
Go back to your grave Jimmy Hill!

Jonathan Lovejoy

584

Nuclear winter waits

For those who choose not to believe

When it will snow ashe and soot

In every part of the Earth

118th Assembly

585

I should like to see the sky

Uncovered by glass

Unframed by wood

Unadorned by the Inevitable

I shall not see the sky again

Uncluttered

The dirt, the grass,

The stones will block my view

586

*G*od is all that there is

All else is illusion

God is the only Truth that exists

Everything else is a lie

587

The quest has been unkind to me

Holding the empty promise

Enticing to pipe dreamery

Whims of prosperity

All the while—in mocking

Take your medicine, if you please!

No cure for your condition

At the bottom of the well

588

I hear the night rain call
Speaking outside my window
Does spring hear the blighted rainfall
On the Eve?

Waiting in the whirlwind
Above the eddy cloud
Too loud to go unheard
Too proud—undeterred

Above clouds of First Heaven
Beneath clouds of Third Heaven
Romadary drips
In the scorching

Jonathan Lovejoy

119th Assembly

589

A song for every bird

And every Bee

Do what you must do

Expediantly

Time is awhine

Down to blowing of the mind

For the tree—as well the flower

Spruce's farewell hour!

590

Above the trees, a new voice calling

The voice of Heaven

Raining the soil

Of broken ground

Voices high above

Beyond what is not meant to be

Voices of Redemption

From Calvary

Jonathan Lovejoy

591

It comes in the evening day

Clothes in the breeze

Bees and butterflies in sleep

Trees whisper prayers to Heaven

The Leavened Bread

To feed a weary traveler

The blood of the Chosen One

Unravels a thirst

In the cool of the evening day

Hopefulness falls astray

To reveal the call from Calvary's Way

In the latter days

592

To commiserate Longfellow's rhyme
A prisoner you will be
Languished til the end of time
Most unwittingly

A rhyming skill to kill your will
Necromantically
Til the valley exalts above the Hill
Retrofrantically

Tethered letters and words together
To fetter a Devil's hand in awe
Verses in guirded brand new leather
Such inspired rhymes as I never saw!

593

*H*eads up, in clouds of mystery!
A Jew—moving through—doth gain
While the voice of doom sounds through creation
When the taboo is unearthed again

Swings and insults, fare thee well!
On the eve of thermonuclear war
Soldiers act in celebration
For the action they've all been waiting for

The Voice of God looms overhead!
Thundering the voice of doom
A clear blue sky—no clouds of dread
Warning wicked choice assumed

594

Offices—the mire

Desire to achieve

In preparation for a crime

At hearshot is cash

Earned under the lash

Much more than one will ever need

Jonathan Lovejoy

595

Others live—

While I die in the rain

Buried under neglect

And ridicule

120th Assembly

596

Demons rule the Land of Dreams
But have no power over the waking mind
Their influence becomes miniscule
Upon the awakening—

Miniature

In the Land where demons rule
Arguments have no foreseeable end
Conflict can never cease
Trouble is spelled with a capital T

Looming always

Storms blow with otherworldly intensity
Sending whirlwinds to doors of safety
The threat of bodily harm is a constant
Along with imprisonment

And death

Elizabethan IV

The Awakening brings a return to sanity
To the other real world
Where demonic presence is felt
But not seen

Where arguments have purpose and function
Conflict carries consequence
Whirlwinds blow terror from the skies
Ineffectively

Human existence itself
Is the world where Satan is King
 In the Land of Dreams
And the Awakening

Jonathan Lovejoy

597

Her eyes burn a yellow flame

Within the walls of prosperity

Shadows threaten to move upon the walls

Choking me in fear

598

Death looms like a storm cloud

Threatening to burst open

To rain a eulogy

So yell, surprise!

Be a good sister

It matters!

They'll let you in if you are

If not, the hot dogs will bite you!

The headache is like a drill

A thrill seeking to kill the stillness of life

And breath

Have hot heavy with peaches and cream

When the aria scar clears up

You can dream again

Just lay there!

Thank heaven you're still alive and healthy

Even though to be born is to be cursed

You've got to take it for what it is…

Life!

If Jesus can do it,

So can you!

So take up your cross

And do the derring do!

There's no need to try not to

You won't be able!

The stable boy said it was alright

He shot Mable!

Then she died in the rain screaming

In too much pain

Pain felt in the bowels of nature

Vowels careening from her mouth into the sky

On a rainy day

Then a sunny day

599

*C*oncerto for the Queen of Berkshire

Behind the walls of prosperity
Grieving for a suffering song to end
A Judge and Queen roam the Hall of Disparity
In dread to see a death march begin

A bereaving shadow of heretofore
Years of prideful malicious strife
Wishing to forget what sins they bore
Days of greed and lust for life

A Queen of Death with regret to spare
In Mourning for two souls to save
Tears cried for empty hearts to bear
Inside the shadow of a lonely grave

600

*D*ance your trolling chord

Roll the rhythm unseen

Rest in the arms of the Lord!

Mice lurk where the corn is green

She strolls the meadow like a flower

Given permission to roam

The milk turned—the sky is sour

Timpanis ensare the gnome!

ABOUT THE AUTHOR

Oscar Lee Whitfield, Jr. is a graduate of the University of North Carolina at Greensboro, with a B.A. in Religious Studies. He currently lives in Winston Salem, North Carolina with his wife, a physical therapist.

For more info on the author's life and career, visit oscarwhitfield.com.